★ The ★
AMERICAN FLAG

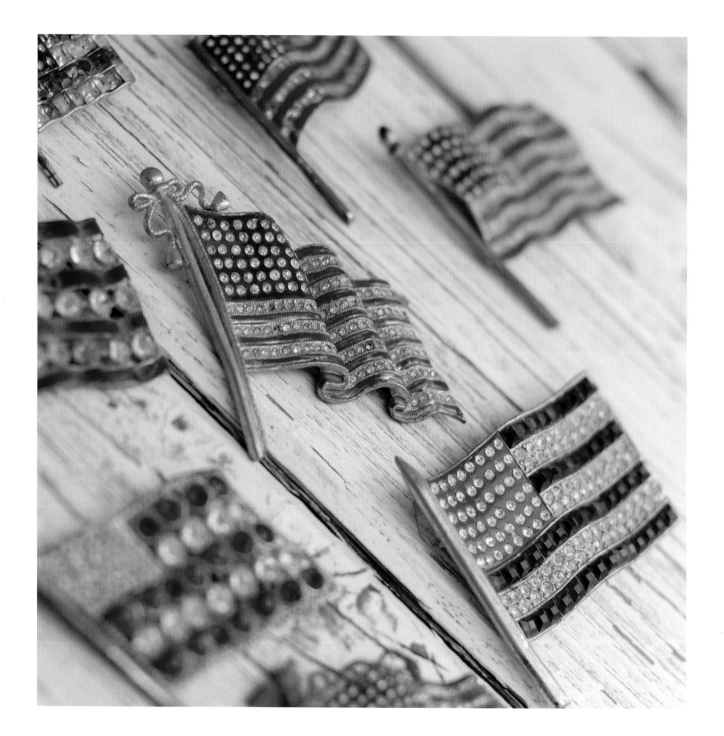

The AMERICAN FLAG

ART, DESIGN FASHION

MARY EMMERLING
PHOTOS BY REED DAVIS

GIBBS SMITH
TO ENRICH AND INSPIRE HUMANKIND

TO
REG JACKSON
SAMANTHA EMMERLING AND NICHOLAS HALL
JONATHAN EMMERLING AND ROSY LUM
TERRY ELLISOR

18 17 16 15 14   5 4 3 2 1

Text © 2014 Mary Emmerling
Photographs © 2014 Reed Davis

Published by
Gibbs Smith
P.O. Box 667
Layton, Utah 84041

1.800.835.4993 orders
www.gibbs-smith.com

Cover design by Michel Vrana
Pages designed by Renee Bond
Printed and bound in Hong Kong

Gibbs Smith books are printed on either recycled, 100% post-consumer waste, FSC-certified papers or on paper produced from sustainable PEFC-certified forest/controlled wood source. Learn more at www.pefc.org.

Library of Congress Control Number: 2013955077

ISBN: 978-1-4236-3647-2

Table of
CONTENTS

Introduction

THE PASSION I HAVE FOR AMERICAN FLAGS

started when I was in public school in Minot, North Dakota, and later in Rehoboth Beach, Delaware. We would gather in the auditorium for exercises that invariably included the recitation of the Pledge of Allegiance and singing of *The Star Spangled Banner*. There was always a special feeling during that time.

This is what flags are all about: the feeling you get in your heart when the president's entourage passes by in a parade or at a cemetery when a flag-draped hearse goes past.

My mother and father are both buried at Arlington National Cemetery. The moment when the guardsmen folded the American flag and handed it to my family was profoundly moving, and I cannot think about it without getting teary-eyed.

And so I collect American flags—both as objects and as visual experiences. Flags and bunting at the World Series, the Fourth of July at the Washington Monument, Rockefeller Center, parades in cities around the country, and sporting and military events. One of my favorite events is the Olympic Games. Seeing our flag waving so proudly among those of other countries is a thrilling sight. I've tried to capture some of these emotions within the collections seen on the pages that follow. I hope they stir something in your heart.

Folk
ART

THE RUSTICITY OF IT IS APPEALING. ITS IMPERFEC-
tions and amateur qualities allow me to feel the artists' passion and spirit through their work. The materials are usually found or natural. People who create folk art often do not think of themselves as artists, so there is a naive exuberance about their pieces.

I started falling in love with folk art the more I visited the folk art museums in New York City and Santa Fe. As I explored, I was drawn to pieces that had flags in or on them: whirligigs, paintings, lathe flags at the beach, quilts, vintage painted gates, hooked rugs, needlework, painted gourds and carved wood. Objects that could be considered as the "art" of the common people.

FACING: Flag by local Hamptons artist Gene Gilligan.

BELOW: This handmade wooden flag (artist unknown) on the side of a beach road serves as a marker for locals and beach-goers.

RIGHT: A lifeguard stand in Amagansett, New York, is the easel for this folk art piece by Long Island artist Gene Gilligan.

FACING: One of Montauk, Long Island's most visible landmarks not only marks where to turn but also proudly bears a homespun symbol of our nation.

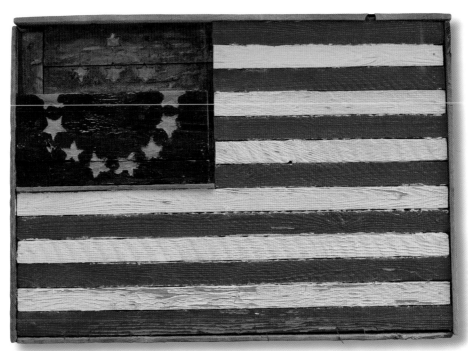

Entrances are a popular place to showcase local artists. The lathe flag at the left is another by Gilligan, at the jitney stop in front of the Huntting Inn, East Hampton.

Many flags were added to the landscape after 9/11, such as this one on the side of a red barn (facing). The Hamptons area is decorated with more flag folk art than any other city I have visited.

FACING: On a building or a car, a painted flag or decal can transform the ordinary into a contemporary statement of pride.

This American fishing dory was used in the early 19th century with a net to do beach fishing for striped bass near the shore (no longer legal). It now sits in front of the Marine Museum in Amagansett.

FACING: Sailor's pocket made out of a torn sail; circa 1850s, depicts two flags with a Navy anchor.

LEFT, ABOVE: Another sailor's pocket sports a picture of a New York–built schooner, circa 1920s.

LEFT AND ABOVE: Vintage flag depictions worked in wool thread.

A life ring encircling a master schooner with eagle overhead and four American flags, circa 1850.

BELOW: Made in wool work by a sailor or a wife at home.

FACING: Made in the Orient for American sailors: an eagle on silk with linen thread, one big flag with white tassels, circa 1890.

Needlework flags: a 1940s tea towel; a 1920s hand-crocheted flag; a 1980s folk art pillow.

Young artist Wyatt Case drew this primitive picture while we were shooting. Love it!

Wooden block art, late 1970s, is by renowned Virginia folk artist Nancy Thomas.

COLLECTIBLES

BARBARA TRUJILLO HAS BEEN AN ANTIQUES
dealer for the past fifty years. She has a collection of turn-of-the-century
American ironstone china complete with flags. While it's hard to find the plates
now, it's nearly impossible to find the pitchers.

Flags can also be found decorating some modern collectible pieces. It is inter-
esting to consider how goods have changed from earlier to modern times. Some
of the same items are made now as then, but they can look completely different.

If you are looking to start a flag collection of your own, here are some ideas
of what to look for: souvenirs, plates, mugs, glassware, china,
games, cigar boxes, tin trays, books, and rarer—
scrimshaw. Happy collecting!

Barbara Trujillo has a fine collection of American ironstone bearing the American flag. The plates, now hard to find, were popular in the early 1900s.

FACING: This was likely an accessory plate, considering its laurel and ribbon decoration and gold border.

White ironstone pitchers circa 1910–40s are very rare now, the flag makes them so valuable. The one at left, with flag and eagle with shield, is one of the rarest of them all.

This rare etched glass is late 1800s.

RIGHT: Vintage mercury vases with the eagle and flag, mid-1800s.

FACING: These china accessory pieces were probably for the dresser or bath. You could use the tall glass vase and cup for tooth brushes, water, or flowers. The little plate would hold rings.

FACING: Scrimshaw was usually made by the sailors at sea for a loved one at home. Brian Trujillo made this scrimshaw folk art in 1973.

Cigar boxes have always been considered collectible. The international and American flag makes this label a desirable piece of art.

Wooden trays made in Brazil: Franklin D. Roosevelt, early 1930s, and United States Merchant Marine.

FACING BELOW: A 1930s reverse-painted glass atop a metal tray with handles—one of my favorites—with the Statue of Liberty, flag and laurel.

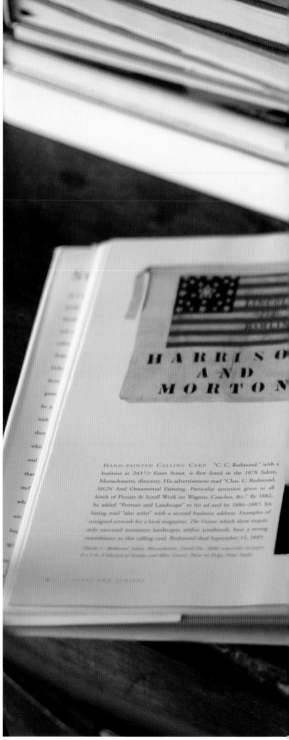

COUNTER-CLOCKWISE FROM TOP: Contemporary flag magnet on the dashboard of a car. • We hung a string of flag lights on a vintage tall pine English clock for a 4th of July party—so festive! • I collect flags of all sorts. Here I've applied a USA decal to a personal travel notebook, and underneath is a postcard of Andy Warhol wrapped in a flag. In the book is a vintage Harrison and Morton political souvenir: Harrison was my great-great-grandfather.

Vintage AMERICANA

DURING MY YOUNG YEARS IN WASHINGTON, DC, and Rehoboth Beach, Delaware, I learned to love the American flag. It seemed to be on display everywhere, from monuments, embassies, parades and museums to the boardwalk, at ride parks, miniature golf and the beach houses in the summer.

When I started collecting antiques in the 1960s, the fad was to purchase things mainly from Europe and Great Britain. Then in 1976, a Bicentennial exhibition at the Whitney Museum in New York City—I think it was called the Flowering of American Antiques— fascinated me. And the American antiques shows really woke me up to purchasing American antiques *only*—especially since I did most of my hunting in New England, where they were old and plentiful.

Here are some charming and vintage items— from souvenirs to toys.

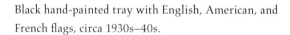

Black hand-painted tray with English, American, and French flags, circa 1930s–40s.

RIGHT: The Coast Guard flew the blue stars with red and white vertical stripes from the mast when launching a ship.

FACING: Framed flag from the stern of a boat, 1940s–50s.

FACING: Toy drum with a gold background, American flag and silver star.

ABOVE: American-made pocket knife, circa 1940, takes a whimsical pose.

ABOVE: Christmas tree ornament, circa 1930.

Vintage games are put to good use by today's collectors in home decorating—on walls, tables, and in baskets. You might be able to find some forgotten gems in an aunty's cupboard or grandma's toy chest.

FACING: "The Game of Flags" card game, circa 1900.

GAME OF FLAGS

Stars and Stripes

PERS...

Denma...
Merchant...

ECUADOR

Stars...

...SIN...

BELGIUM

UNITED STATES.

Washington designed our glorious banner. The red and white stripes represent the thirteen original States. Red denotes daring, force defiance; and white, purity. The stars represent the present Union. The blue ground was taken from the Covenanters' banner of Scotland, and signifies vigilance, perseverance, justice. It is worn at the main of ships, and in the bows of boats, when the President of the United States is on board.

GREAT BRITAIN—MAN-OF-WAR.

For a long time the distinguishing flag of England has been a white flag with a red cross, which is a sign of crusades. In the canton is the "Union Jack," so-called from James I. (Jacques), in whose reign it was constructed.

HAYTI.

These col...

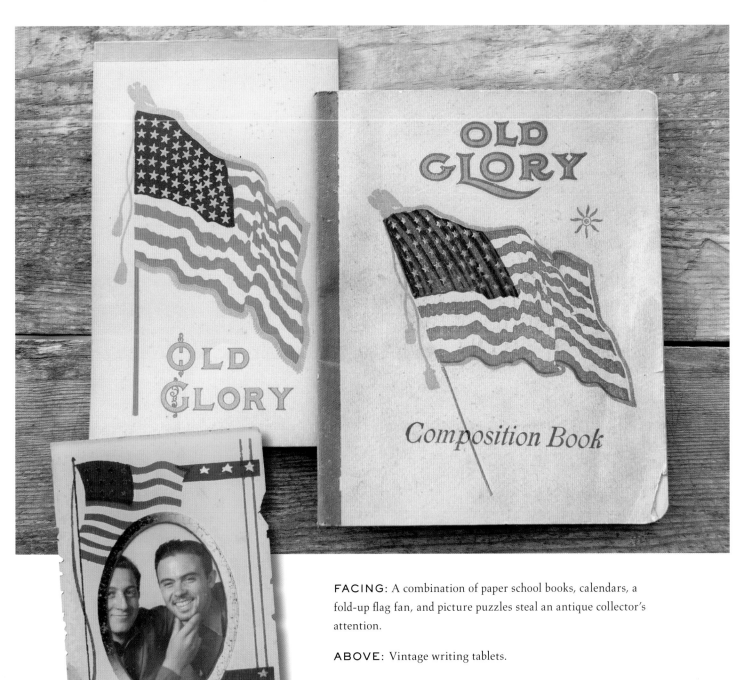

FACING: A combination of paper school books, calendars, a fold-up flag fan, and picture puzzles steal an antique collector's attention.

ABOVE: Vintage writing tablets.

LEFT: A glass picture frame, circa 1920s.

ABOVE: Stuffed fabric Navy doll, 1920s.

RIGHT: Die-cast Uncle Sam, circa 1930.

FACING: Metal toy soldiers on stands 1930s–40s.

FACING: A paper plaque, long may it wave; tiny framed American flag; 1920s metal cricket toy.

ABOVE: Metal Uncle Sam silhouette stands guard in a garden.

LEFT: Turn-of-the-century child's tin beach bucket.

★ 53 ★

ABOVE: Very old American flag ribbons in silk and satin.

RIGHT: Rare soldier and bride cake topper.

FACING: Two wooden flags surrounding a life ring with a clipper in the middle, 1850s. The Japanese made these to sell to the soldiers. If the ship was in the harbor long enough, they would paint the sailor's ship on them.

FACING AND LEFT: Flag decal on a 1920s vintage metal tray.

BELOW LEFT: Vintage flag fabric made into a door hanger.

BELOW: A homemade fabric potpourri bag with fringe.

Victory and PATRIOTISM

IT IS ALWAYS A SPECIAL MOMENT TO WEAR OR
display a flag in honor of a war victory or other occasion of patriotic pride.

Vintage patriotic pins have been popular particularly during wartime—World War II, for instance. There were V for victory pins, remember Pearl Harbor pins, women's auxiliary pins and more. Enamel-painted metal was common for lapel pins worn by veterans and military members. Soldiers would also send sweetheart pins to their loves back home.

There were patriotic shields in plastic, metal and glass with sparkling rhinestones in brilliant colors. One of my personal favorites is the Uncle Sam brooch.

The flags on these jewelry pieces evoke a period in time when people felt united through the common cause of patriotism.

Vintage painted metal pins.

FACING: A mix of enameled metal and rhinestone pins—flags, hats, shields, and eagles.

As small as these pins are, they feature very fine details.

LEFT, TOP TO BOTTOM: Enameled pin for remembering Pearl Harbor. Uncle Sam's hat political pin. Waving flag political pin with tassels, 1950s.

TOP: Eagle pin with two American flags crossed at the poles.

ABOVE: Silver marcasite eagle carrying an enameled flag, 1940s.

ABOVE: Vintage rhinestone eagle.

RIGHT: A collection of victory pins—New York, British and American, and a gold eagle with rhinestones.

FACING, CLOCKWISE FROM TOP LEFT: Enameled bow pin. Patriotic eagle with a shield charm. W for Wilkie. Silver link bracelet with enameled flags, early 1940s. Victory pin in rhinestones.

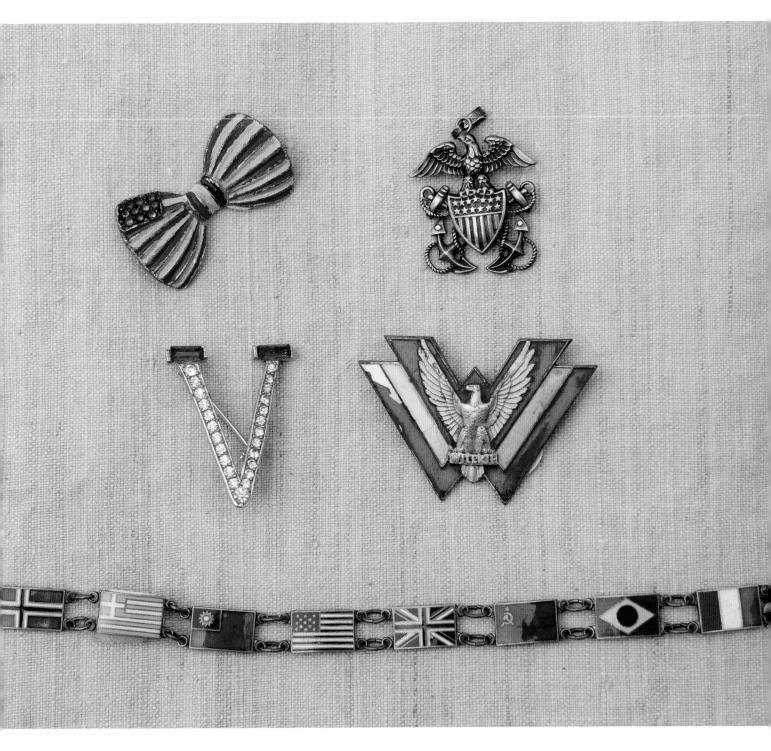

LEFT, CLOCKWISE FROM V: All are pins: silver victory; enameled eagle; red rhinestone airplane; enamel bow with rhinestones; God Bless America metal eagle; aqua, clear, and red liberty bell; Caduceus with spread eagles wings in enamel with a large blue rhinestone on top.

ABOVE: Women's World War II auxiliary pin.

RIGHT: Enameled 13-star flag on a stick.

Two if BY SEA

SMALL PRIMITIVE PAINTINGS ARE SOME OF MY
treasured collections. Most of them are depictions of the water and the ocean done by locals living on the East Coast from the 1950s–70s. I really get excited if I find one that includes something more—a flagpole, lighthouse, or country cottage.

I also buy paintings for their frames. Frames that are hand-carved, ornate, solid wood and original are functional and handsome items in a painting collection.

I frequent historical societies and museums looking for beach and boating scenes and, of course, photos that include flags. Black-and-white photographs also add vintage and beauty to my collection.

Brian Trujillo has been a commercial fisherman his whole life. He has been collecting for more than 40 years and specializes in ship paintings dated 1875–1920. Ship paintings are hard to find and expensive nowadays, he says. The paintings that follow are from his collection.

RIGHT: A wooden yacht.

BELOW AND FACING:
Tugboats, steady and reliable.
They still help ships out of the
harbors today.

*"Oh, it's home again, and
home again, America for me!*

*I want a ship that's westward
bound to plough the rolling
sea,*

*To the blessed Land of Room
Enough beyond the ocean bars,*

*Where the air is full of sun-
light and the flag is full of
stars."*

—from "America for Me," by
Henry Van Dyke

RIGHT: Kate Moffatt watercolor. *Tugboat on the Great Lakes* has a very big American flag.

BELOW: The tug boat *Powow* in the Boston Harbor; oil on board.

KATE MOFFATT.

ABOVE LEFT: Clipper ship; oil on board.

ABOVE RIGHT: A wool work piece made by an American sailor. The thread was made from old wool clothing. Here, a clipper ship is encircled by a wreath of six flags.

LEFT: Flags stand out against the black-and-white ship, displayed in an antique mahogany frame.

LEFT: On the wall, top left, a sail schooner; painting by William Pierce Stubbs. Top right, Japanese-made reprints on paper of original oil paintings, sold to sailors as souvenirs. Below those is a House of Flags of various Nantucket whaling ships circa 1850.

BELOW: Seven-masted schooner, probably in New England.

FACING: *Pilot Boat 17*, oil painting by Antonio Nicolo Jacobsen, New York boat.

Our flag is the national ensign, pure and simple . . . Behold it! Listen to it! Every star has a tongue, every stripe is articulate.

—Robert C. Winthrop

ABOVE: Sailboats out in the ocean with seagulls; on land, a lighthouse and a cottage, early 1900s. The flag is very small in this painting.

FACING, TOP LEFT: Historical photo, Miami, 1920s.

FACING, TOP RIGHT AND BOTTOM: Paintings I have collected over 40 years: beach cottage with an American flag, and a primitive painting with a country house, orange lighthouse, and a flag on a very wide pole.

JEWELRY

EVERY WOMAN HAS FAVORITE PIECES OF JEWELRY.
Among mine are a flag belt buckle, a beaded Native American leather cuff bracelet, and so many wonderful rhinestone flags, as well as bald eagle pins.

The thing about jewelry is, you can wear one piece or ten—whatever you
can handle. Or you can attach pins to a purse. My jewelry pieces also do double
duty as home décor. I like to have favorite antiques or objects that are part of a
collection on display, to please my eye and for others to see when they come to
my home. I like to create a wall display by putting several pieces together on a
background fabric.

Flags—especially ones that appear to be waving in the breeze—set a festive
and patriotic mood. Twenty years ago I acquired a God Bless
America charm bracelet. What an exciting find! It's
fun collecting all the different kinds of
Americana jewelry.

A wonderful collection of vintage rhinestone American flag-on-pole pins, mostly 1940s. My favorites have the very large round or square stones.

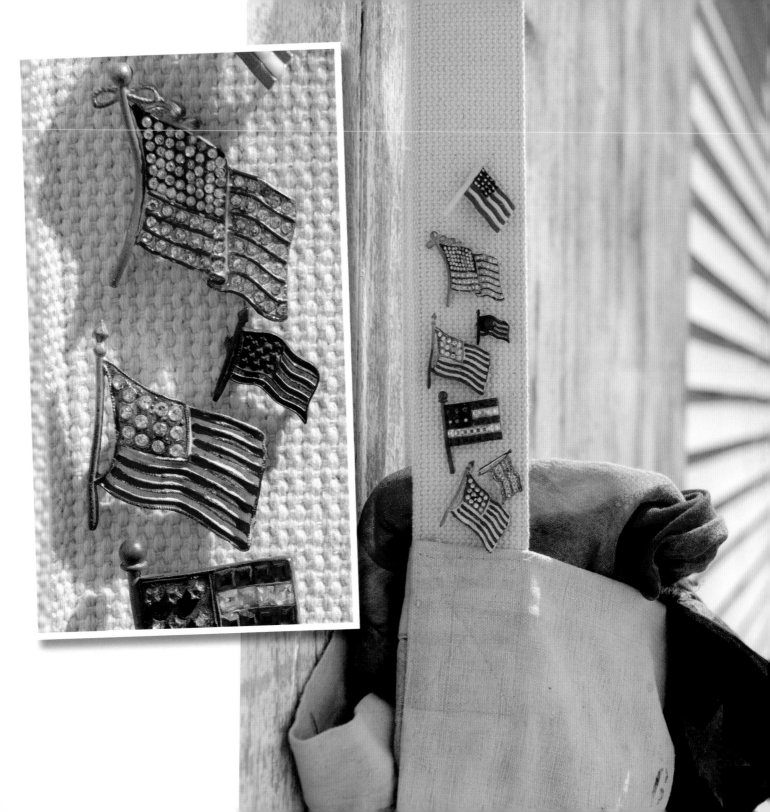

"We take the stars from heaven, the red from our mother country, separating it by white stripes, thus showing that we have separated from her, and the white stripes shall go down to posterity, representing our liberty."

—attributed to George Washington

"I am the clutch of an idea, and the reasoned purpose of reso-lution. I am no more than you believe me to be and I am all that you believe I can be."

—Franklin Knight Lane

FACING: God Bless America 1940s plastic bracelet was also available as a necklace.

ABOVE: A 1950s rhinestone bracelet and matching ring.

FAR LEFT: Three-string bracelet with a fancy rhinestone clasp.

LEFT: Bakelite pin, WWII era.

Clothing and ACCESSORIES

PIECES OF CLOTHING THAT I REALLY LOVE ARE usually on display somewhere in my house if I'm not wearing them. Scarves are especially good for bringing texture and color into a room.

Of all the scarves I own, the American flag scarves are my most-liked. I have small flag bandanas, which I sometimes tie around my dog Olive's neck, and a cotton one is tied around my suitcase handle. When I wear my vintage Levi's jean jacket, I almost always wear a long flag scarf with it. It makes me feel like a proud American, but at the same time I am still a country girl at heart.

To find flag clothing and accessories, I look in good stores, drug stores, fun stores, antique stores, and even dollar stores.

From cowboy boots to jackets, hats and totes, good old stars and stripes decorate the things we wear and that make us feel comfy.

The small antique fabric flags on a stick pin were for the lapel, to show support for the war.

RIGHT: Vintage belt buckle with an enamel waving flag.

FACING: My favorite cell phone cover!

The colors of patriotism are evident in every corner of fashion, from bags to key chains and cowboy boots.

A commemorative interpretation, 1776–1976, with turquoise where the stars would be.

FACING: A vintage cotton handkerchief. The song is the "Star Spangled Banner."

FACING: Curly, the dog, dons a favorite scarf.

ABOVE: Cotton bunting fabric circa 1915, used for political events.

RIGHT: I love all kinds of flag scarves, from bandanas, silk, and cotton to fringed wool.

It's always fun to wear festive red, white and blue—bathing suits no exception! I made full pants from the vintage bunting fabric to wear on summer celebration days, especially the Fourth of July.

Beaded key chains
made by Native
Americans.

Beaded American flags on a
leather bracelet, circa 1950; a contemporary necklace from the Santa
Fe Spanish Market; and leather
riding gloves.

Flags on outerwear, including a denim jacket that has been worn forever.

On DISPLAY

THERE ARE TOWNS ALL OVER THE COUNTRY THAT are charming and picturesque, where holidays are celebrated as a community. The Hamptons, where I lived for 35 years, is one such area, and the Fourth of July is the highlight of summer.

As I drove around my hometown and various others, I observed that the tradition of flying the American flag is alive and well. There were flags attached to motorcycles, boats and houses; waving from churches, museums, porches, and even the wharf. There were flags everywhere I went—in the country and in the towns.

At my home, I have vintage 45-star flags in frames and antique flags hanging from poles leaning in corners of various rooms. Outside my house, there is always a flag flying when we are home, and it means that people are welcome to stop by!

Outside and indoors, flags are prominent in the landscape of American décor.

Summer in Santa Barbara. The flag I spotted behind a pink Thing was one of my favorites, because I used to have a yellow Thing. Next to it, a cute Vespa. A motorcyclist downtown proudly displayed multiple flags on his ride.

From trucks to lifeguard stands, the flag is everywhere in summer.

In country settings, particularly, the flag seems perfectly at home as decor.

"I am whatever you make me, nothing more. I am your belief in yourself, your dream of what a people may become . . ."
—Franklin Knight Lane

Why do flags and lobsters make us think of summer?

FACING: Sag Harbor, New York, recognizes veterans, who have given us freedom.

. . . on the dock of the bay . . . in Sag Harbor.

"You're the emblem of / The land I love. / The home of the free and the brave."

—George M. Cohan

Flags on display in home settings: a framed long 13-star; a 50-star flag blowing in the breeze; a 48-star cotton in a black frame, 1896–1907; and a wonderful vintage wool 13-star, facing.

"The colors of the pales (the vertical stripes) are those used in the flag of the United States of America; White signifies purity and innocence, Red, hardiness and valour, and Blue, the color of the Chief (the broad band above the stripes) signifies vigilance, perseverance and justice."

—The Great Seal of the United States

I like surprises—seeing a flag hanging between two trees, off the front of a porch, or on top of a shed.

One of the biggest wool flags I have seen, 8 x 10 feet. You can hang a flag anywhere for a special occasion.

Flags affixed to your bicycle make you feel like a kid riding in a parade, no matter what your age.

Small flags for celebrations at home.

In memoriam . . .

A special afternoon in September at a cemetery in Wainscott, Long Island.

Picnic
AND PATIO

OUTDOOR DECORATING IS GREAT FUN! FOR MY
American country store in East Hampton, I had made a red, white, and blue flag
gate for the entrance to the barn, which we became famous for.

Wrapping a flag scarf around a garden statue; poking stick flags through-
out the garden, in planters, and in fresh flower arrangements; laying flag beach
towels on the chaise lounge or hanging them from peg racks
near the outdoor shower and pool area are some ways to add
personality to the outdoors.

Things I pick up for outdoors are flag mugs,
metal tins with stars and stripes, candles in all
shapes and size and many novelty items. Don't
forget to look for sparklers, glitter, tissue
paper and napkins. Always be ready to
celebrate with red, white and blue!

An old fabric-covered brick doorstop; holiday twisted licorice candy.

Perfect for summer: a luscious red, white and blueberry dessert served in an antique dish.

"You're a grand old flag / You're a high flying flag / And forever in peace may you wave."
—George M. Cohan

Classic decorations and accoutrements for a summer picnic.

FACING: A vintage decorative fan decorates an outdoor space.

"That piece of red, white and blue bunting means five thousand years of struggle upwards. It is the full-grown flower of ages of fighting for liberty. It is the century plant of human hope in bloom."

—Alvin Owsley

RESOURCES

Ann Lawrence

927 Baca Street

Santa Fe, NM 87505

505.982.1755

annlawrencecollection.com

Back at the Ranch

209 E. Marcy Street

Santa Fe, NM 87501

505.989.8110

Backattheranch.com

Barbara Trujillo

2466 Main Street

Bridgehampton, NY 11932

631.537.3838

Bizerk

432 State Street

Santa Barbara, CA 93101

805.252.5037

Bungalow

15330 N. Hayden, Suite 120

Scottsdale, AZ 85260

480.948.5409

Bungalowfurniture.com

Camps and Cottages

1233 N. Coast Hwy

Laguna Beach, CA 92651

949.494.2100

camps-cottages.com

Country Heart Antiques

Sandra J. Whitson

P.O. Box 272

Lititz, PA 17543

717.626.4978

npknring@ptd.net

Gone Local

80 N. Main Street

East Hampton, NY 11937

631.267.5315

gonelocalamagansett.com

John Varvatos

54 Newton Lane

East Hampton, NY 11937

631.324.4440

Johnvarvatos.com

Juxtaposition Home

7976 E. Coast Hwy

Newport Beach, CA 92657

949.715.1181

juxtapositionhome.com

Marburger Farm Antique Show

407 W. 7th Street

Tyler, TX 75701

800.947.5799

Ashley@marburgershow.com

Marine Museum

301 Bluff Road

Amagansett, NY 11930

631.267.6544

Melet Mercantile

84 Wooster Street #205

New York, NY 10012

212.925.8353

Meletmercantile.com

The Monogram shop

7 Newtown Lane

East Hampton, NY 11937

631.329.3379

themonogramshops.com

Nathalie

503 Canyon Road

Santa Fe, NM 87501

505.982.1021

nathaliesantafe.com

Pijnappels

39 S. Main

Casnovia, MI 49318

616.675.5481

pijnapples@aol.com

Rachel Ashwell

Couture Prairie

5808 Wagner Road

Round Top, TX 78954

979.836.4975

rachelashwellshabbychiccouture.com

Rooms and Gardens

924 State Street

Santa Barbara, CA 93101

805.965.2424

Roomsandgardens.com

Round Top Antiques Fair

P.O. Box 180

Smithville, TX 78957

502.237.4747

Roundtoptexasantiques.com

RRL

57 Main Street

East Hampton, NY 11937

631.907.9201

Sweet Salvage

4648 N. 7th Avenue

Phoenix, AZ 85013

602.279.2996

Sweetsalvage.net

A Wilder Place in Time

2213 Lakeway Terrace

Flower Mound, TX 75028

972.342.8776

Lindat.Wilder@verizon.net

Acknowledgments

A BIG SPECIAL THANKS TO BARBARA TRUJILLO, WHO
taught me how to collect and has been inspiring me for over 30 years.

Brian Trujillo

Patti Kenner

Brian Ramaekers and his dog, Curly

Michael and Jolie Kelter

Jean Brooks

Carol Glasser

John & Laurie Sykes

Wendy Lane

Ann Lawrence

Wyatt Case

Bob Kaplan, Pedego Bikes

Gene Gilligan

Dorine Drohan

Sue Seitz-Kulick

Carly Homer

Madge Baird, a great and talented editor

Michel Vrana for a great cover design

Renee Bond for beautiful pages

A big thank-you to Reed Davis, whose photography always makes me feel great.

THANK YOU TO MARY EMMERLING, NOT ONLY FOR THE
privilege of working together for years but that we have become friends in the process.

—Reed Davis